THE LITTLE BOOK OF

ARSENAL
LEGENDS

Independent and Unofficial

First published in 2025 by OH
An Imprint of HEADLINE PUBLISHING GROUP LIMITED

1

Disclaimer:

ISBN 978-1-03542-288-3

Compiled and written by: David Clayton
Editorial: Chris Stone and Matt Tomlinson
Designed and typeset in Helvetica Now by: Tony Seddon
Project manager: Russell Porter
Production: Arlene Lestarde
Printed and bound in Dubai

HEADLINE PUBLISHING GROUP LIMITED
An Hachette UK Company
Carmelite House, 50 Victoria Embankment, London EC4Y 0DZ

The authorised representative in the EEA is Hachette Ireland, 8 Castlecourt Centre, Dublin 15, D15 XTP3, Ireland (email: info@hbgi.ie)

www.headline.co.uk   www.hachette.co.uk

THE LITTLE BOOK OF

ARSENAL LEGENDS

Independent and Unofficial

THE GREATEST PLAYERS TO WEAR THE SHIRT
AND THE GREATEST MANAGERS TO LEAD THE TEAM

CONTENTS

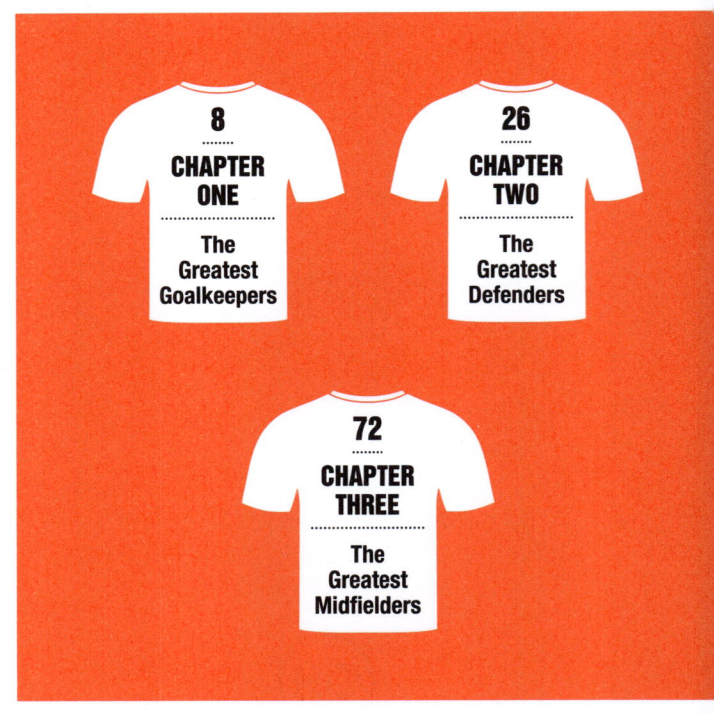

INTRODUCTION

Founded in December 1886, Arsenal Football Club are historically one of English football's biggest and most successful teams. With a fanbase that spreads far and wide across the globe, the Gunners have experienced more success than most and have enjoyed many glorious eras, won countless trophies and had some truly wonderful players wear the famous red shirt with white sleeves.

With almost 50 major trophies won, the North London side have remained a powerhouse domestically, and while a Champions League title has so far eluded the club, it feels only a matter of time before Arsenal end that long wait – and maybe repeat the historic feats of the Invincibles team.

Gunners club legends are numerous, from goalkeeping giants like Pat Jennings and David Seaman to defensive colossuses like Tony Adams, Martin Keown and William Saliba.

In midfield, there have been magical talents such

as Liam Brady, Martin Ødegaard and Patrick Vieira, while the strikers have included such luminaries as Cliff Bastin, Ian Wright and Dennis Bergkamp.

Including a selection of managerial geniuses, in the pages that follow you'll discover the players and managers that have stood out and remained in the memories of those lucky enough to have seen them. From the good old days to the here and now, *The Little Book of Arsenal Legends* showcases the giants that have made this football club what it is today.

CHAPTER

1

THE GREATEST GOALKEEPERS

Keeping goal for the Gunners, there have been some fantastic custodians who have worn the No. 1 jersey.

While each had their own areas of excellence, the four in this chapter are considered the greatest ever to wear that coveted No. 1 jersey...

Bob Wilson
1963 – 1974

Bob Wilson had to bide his time to become Arsenal No. 1. Though he joined the club in 1963, it would be five years before the hardworking Scot would be given the chance to establish himself – something he would do for the next six seasons at Highbury. Wilson was a fearless keeper, his strength saving at opposition players' feet – a trait that would see him sustain a lot of injures in his line of duty.

A fantastic club servant, he was voted the Arsenal Player of the Year in the unforgettable 1970–71 "Double"-winning campaign.

GAMES

League 234

FA Cup 32

League Cup 18

Europe 24

Other 0

Total **308**

TROPHIES

First Division x 1

FA Cup x 1

Inter Cities Fairs Cup x 1

Specialised coaching of this kind is crucial, to my mind, and I regret that it wasn't available to me during my time as a player. I worked with Bob Wilson towards the end of my time at Arsenal, but, apart for that, such coaching was rare.

PAT JENNINGS

In a one-on-one against goalkeepers I would bet on myself every time. This is the only time I can remember a keeper getting the better of me. I cannot believe it.

GEORGE BEST

We were hard back then. We'd kick each other on purpose and it was rough. It was brutal.

BOB WILSON

I've got scars all over my head, two artificial hips. I had dislocated fingers, broken ribs, torn cartilage, dislocated shoulder, broken elbow – but the thing that made me stand out was my ability to dive head first at the feet of an attacker. It was my trademark.

BOB WILSON

Pat Jennings
1977 – 1985

When it comes to legendary Arsenal goalkeepers, few can eclipse Pat Jennings. The Northern Ireland international seamlessly joined the Gunners from Tottenham Hotspur and – despite his connections – would become equally popular on the other side of North London. Able to pluck crosses into the box with consummate ease, he was also a formidable presence in one-on-one situations, as well as being blessed with razor sharp reflexes.

Jennings appeared in three successive FA Cup finals in the late 1970s and served the club with great distinction for eight years. A giant in both physicality and reputation.

GAMES

League 237
FA Cup 29
League Cup 11
Europe 19
Other.................................1
Total **297**

TROPHIES

FA Cup x 1

Pat Jennings was the most natural goalkeeper I had the pleasure of working with. When he joined Arsenal, aged 31, I spent 10 years working with him and I taught him nothing. Jennings does credit me with keeping his desire going to keep playing, which he did until his 41st birthday, so I did have some impact on him.

BOB WILSON

Pat's save left me wondering how he had got to the ball. I burst through with half a dozen players behind me, and I had to shoot quickly. I really caught the shot just right and it was going over Pat's right shoulder as he came out. I could hear the crowd behind the goal, stretching right up into the Kop, shouting 'goal' – but there was the ball in Pat's hands. It was amazing. One of the finest saves I've seen in my life.

STEVE HEIGHWAY

Some of the young keepers think they shouldn't make mistakes. The man who doesn't make mistakes, he hasn't been born yet. It's the ones that make the fewest mistakes that are the best goalkeepers.

PAT JENNINGS

I knew at Arsenal, I was playing with two or three old boys in the international team, Pat Rice and Sammy Nelson. I knew all the other Irish lads, it was home from home, basically. It meant, from my point of view, that I didn't have to move the family or the kids out of London.

PAT JENNINGS

David Seaman
1990 – 2003

With more than 13 years' service as Arsenal No. 1, 12 trophies won and 564 appearances, it's no wonder many consider David Seaman to have been the Gunners' greatest goalkeeper.

The amiable Yorkshireman arrived from QPR in 1990 and would make the keeper's shirt his own throughout one of the club's most successful eras. Seaman was nicknamed "Safe Hands" for good reason – he was steady, reliable with a calm temperament that gave the defenders in front of him confidence and assurance.

Revered by Arsenal fans, he fully deserves his status as a Gunners legend.

GAMES

League 405
FA Cup 48
League Cup 38
Europe 67
Other 6
Total **564**

TROPHIES

First Division/Premier League x 3
FA Cup x 4
League Cup x 1
FA Charity/Community Shield x 3

European Cup Winners' Cup x 1

The best goalkeeper I've seen is David Seaman. He won nine major trophies at Arsenal, and he was just phenomenal. With over 1,000 appearances in the game, he is a real great. What I found amazing was that he could be talking to a ball boy or a man in the crowd only 10 seconds before kick-off, just having a laugh and giggling, but as soon as that whistle went he was 'in the zone' as they say. David was amazing.

BOB WILSON

I still think John Lukic is one of the top three keepers in the country. I just think David Seaman is the best.

GEORGE GRAHAM

Massive, massive mentality. The mental strength, you've just got to have that because you get a lot of stick, as a goalkeeper you're the last line of defence. When a goal goes in everyone looks at you, you've got to be able to deal with that. If you make a mistake, it could be a bad mistake, how are you going to recover? Are you going to react positively or are you just going to cave in?

DAVID SEAMAN

I've always liked long hair. My dad's always had long hair, but he always tells me, 'I never had it in a ponytail.' And I say to him, 'You weren't an England goalie either, were ya?'

DAVID SEAMAN

Jens Lehmann
2003 – 2008 and 2011

Colourful imposing and sometimes controversial, Jens Lehmann kept goal for Arsenal for five years. During his time at Highbury and the Emirates, Lehmann was very much in the mould of the Peter Schmeichel school of goalkeeping,

The German international was a formidable presence who would do whatever was necessary to keep the ball out of his net. The fact that he was also tasked with replacing David Seaman and was ever-present during his first campaign – the "Invincibles season" – is reason enough to consider Lehmann as a Gunner great. After leaving in 2008, he returned in 2011 to play one more game as emergency cover – his 200th and last for the club.

GAMES

League 148
FA Cup 13
League Cup 0
Europe 36
Other 3
Total **200**

TROPHIES

Premier League x 1
FA Cup x 1
FA Community Shield x 1

The goalkeeper gets more pressure and more criticism when he lets a goal in. You have seen that recently with England. But I want to make it clear I have 100 per cent faith in Jens Lehmann.

ARSÈNE WENGER

Jens is trying every day to make life difficult for those who compete with him. That is very good because it makes those who are competing with him improve as well. He is a 100 per cent professional. He gives something to the team as well in the dressing room if it is needed.

ARSÈNE WENGER

At Arsenal we play a very attractive, offensive style so I always have to be aware of counter attacks when you have to shift your position a lot more.

JENS LEHMANN

Arsenal have a goalkeeper emergency at the moment. I'll gladly step in.

JENS LEHMANN

CHAPTER
2

THE GREATEST DEFENDERS

Arsenal have taken great pride over the years in their reputation for tough, no-nonsense defending. The old song, "1–0 to the Arsenal" is still sung today with reverence to the defensive giants of the past...

Kenny Sansom
1980 – 1988

For eight seasons, Kenny Sansom served Arsenal with great distinction and, for a time, was arguably the best left-back in Europe.

Joining the Gunners in 1980 from Crystal Palace, he was a remarkably consistent defender. Sansom had one spell where he missed just seven games in all competitions over six seasons, going on to captain the team. He would also go on to win 88 caps for England when he was the national team's chosen left-back for almost a decade. A fantastic, classy and reliable defender.

GAMES and GOALS

League	314	6
FA Cup	26	0
League Cup	2	0
Europe	0	0
Other	54	0
Total	**394**	**6**

TROPHIES

League Cup x 1

Kenny was my hero; I was so pleased I joined Arsenal and got to play with him.

LEE DIXON

My first impression of young Kenny Sansom was, 'You might not be very tall son, but you've got the body of a middleweight boxer with determination and guts to match.' He was 16 years old, short and stocky with tremendous upper-body power. But it was his lightning pace that made him one of the best left-backs of all time.

TERRY VENABLES

Arsenal are a great club. Where do you go from Arsenal?

KENNY SANSOM

I was ushered quickly through the door leading into the East Stand before being taken to see Ken Friar over in the West Stand. It was all very impressive for a young impressionable lad like me and I was flattered when I was asked if I wanted to play for the Arsenal. Was he having a laugh? 'That would be terrific,' I gulped.

KENNY SANSOM

Tony Adams
1983 – 2002

When your nickname is Mr Arsenal, you know you must be doing something right! Homegrown centre-back Tony Adams spent 14 years as Arsenal captain and made an incredible 672 appearances during that time, winning 10 major honours in three different decades.

A one-club man, Adams committed himself to the Gunners' cause in every way imaginable. Along with centre-back partner Steve Bould and full-backs Lee Dixon and Nigel Winterburn, he was the glue that helped shape the famous "Back Four" into the meanest and most efficient defence unit in English football – if not of all time. A natural leader, Adams was fearless and fearsome, rarely beaten in the air or on the ground. One of the club's greatest players.

GAMES and GOALS

League	504	32
FA Cup	54	8
League Cup	59	5
Europe	48	3
Other	7	1
Total	**672**	**49**

TROPHIES

First Division/Premier League x 4

FA Cup x 3

League Cup x 2

FA Charity Shield x 2

European Cup Winners' Cup x 1

When I first came to Arsenal, I realised the back four were all university graduates in the art of defending. As for Tony Adams, I consider him to be a doctor of defence. He is simply outstanding.

ARSÈNE WENGER

He was just brilliant. He was a great man-motivator, knew when to get on your back, but knew when to do it, when you needed a little shove. Just a great captain and it was great having him in front of me.

DAVID SEAMAN

I was the captain of the club so I made sure
that I bullied basically everyone else.

TONY ADAMS

When I finished up at Arsenal in 2002, aged 36,
I was asked if I fancied a season at Rangers, but I
would have just been picking up money. Besides I
wanted to be remembered as a one-club man.

TONY ADAMS

Martin Keown
1984 – 1986 and 1993 – 2004

Though he may not have initially felt the love of the Arsenal fans, over time that would change – and then some. Keown struggled to find his feet in his early days at Highbury, and was surprisingly allowed to join Aston Villa aged 20, but he would return seven years later to eventually partner Tony Adams. They would forge an equally formidable defensive shield, while his ferocious appetite for physical duels made him one of the most feared opponents for any number of Premier League strikers.

   His second spell lasted almost a dozen years, and if he'd felt he had unfinished business with the Gunners, by the time he left, he'd more than fulfilled his dreams.

GAMES and GOALS

League	332	4
FA Cup	40	0
League Cup	23	1
Europe	49	3
Other	5	0
Total	**449**	**8**

TROPHIES

Premier League x 3

FA Cup x 3

FA Charity/Community Shield x 3

European Cup Winners' Cup x 1

Martin was an old fashioned man-to-man defender. I played against him numerous times and he was very difficult to play against, because if you're his man, that's it, he'll follow you everywhere. He'd follow you if you went for a wee!

PERRY GROVES

Martin loves what he does, and he's ready for the fight to win. It's an attitude that rubs off on the younger players.

ARSÈNE WENGER

If anyone asks me about Tony Adams, I always think I'm a better player than him. People will say that is ridiculous, but no, no, no. I genuinely thought I was a better defender.

MARTIN KEOWN

There was a tremendous desire and passion to pull away the stranglehold that [Manchester] United had on English football – and this group of players were capable of doing it.

MARTIN KEOWN

William Saliba

2019 – present day

It's fair to say that when Arsenal signed 18-year-old William Saliba from Saint-Etienne in 2019, the deal slipped under the radar somewhat. In fact, over the next three seasons, Saliba returned on loan to France with Saint-Etienne, then spent a season each with Nice and Marseille.

He returned to the Emirates for the 2022–23 season and, after making his debut against Crystal Palace, the talented centre-back has never looked back. Considered one of the best defenders in world football, Saliba has forged a formidable partnership with Gabriel to provide a foundation for the Gunners' Premier League title attempts. Strong, quick and intelligent, Saliba has quickly become one of the club's best young defenders since Tony Adams.

GAMES and GOALS*

League	86	6
FA Cup	3	0
League Cup	4	0
Europe	20	1
Other	1	0
Total	**114**	**7**

* as of 31/01/2025

TROPHIES

FA Community Shield x 1

He came back and after one or two training sessions, in a new environment, we knew that, from now on, he could do it. Since, he has proved that brilliantly. His progression and his consistency are incredible. We are very happy to have him here.

MIKEL ARTETA

William Saliba is currently the best young defender in the world and can go on to be the best defender in the world. He has everything to get better and better. I remember Tony Adams when he was young – he might make quite a few mistakes, but he always seemed to rectify them. Saliba's got his opportunity now and he's not let anybody down – Arsenal are very lucky to have him, and he could become a club legend.

RAY PARLOUR

I want to win everything possible here,
and to put the club back on the very top.
I want to win every title.

WILLIAM SALIBA

It makes a big difference to have fans like
we do. In the bad moments they help us and we
always want to say thank you through what we do
on the pitch and try to win the game for them.
We play football for this. You play for the fans, you
play for the good moments, and you play for
that feeling at the Emirates.

WILLIAM SALIBA

Gabriel Magalhães

2020 – present day

After signing for Arsenal in September 2020, Gabriel steadily established himself in the starting XI before becoming one of the first names on the team-sheet. The Brazilian defender, like central partner William Saliba, is aggressive, commanding and quick, and the partnership is considered one of – if not the – best in Europe.

Gabriel has become a rock of the Arsenal back line and undoubtedly his star will continue to rise. He also has a habit of scoring important goals and is as threatening as any striker in set-piece situations. A modern-day legend in the making.

GAMES and GOALS*

League	153	17
FA Cup	5	1
League Cup	11	0
Europe	28	2
Other	1	0
Total	**198**	**20**

* as of 31/01/2025

TROPHIES

FA Community Shield x 1

A lot of things have happened to him. His role in the team has grown. His personal life is also very different to the one he had before, with his family and his language. He also changed a lot of things in his life and improved his mentality. He can decide what he wants to be and I think he made the right call to take the direction he took.

MIKEL ARTETA

I love him, he loves me, so it's easier to play.

WILLIAM SALIBA

Whenever I hear my own song as well… wow, it's incredible. I'm so happy about that – it's a dream for me. I always want to thank the Gunners fans for that, because I love it. I think it was my wife who heard it first on social media. She was so happy too.

GABRIEL

Here, how we play, how we stick together, how we work for each other – I've never seen this anywhere else before. It's a dream for me to be a part of it.

GABRIEL

David O'Leary

1975 – 1993

David O'Leary sits comfortably among a pantheon of Arsenal legends. His 18 years at Highbury saw him make an incredible 722 appearances, win numerous trophies and serve the club he loved with great distinction during three different decades.

A football-playing centre-back, O'Leary was deceptively strong for his slender physique, strong in the air and quick. The softly-spoken Irishman would go on to captain the Gunners for a period of time before injuries began to make his appearances more sporadic towards the end of his illustrious career. A wonderfully cultured defender and a fantastic club servant, he will be forever considered a club legend.

GAMES and GOALS

League	558	11
FA Cup	70	1
League Cup	70	2
Europe	20	0
Other	4	0
Total	**722**	**14**

TROPHIES

First Division x 2
FA Cup x 2
League Cup x 2
FA Charity Shield x 1

David didn't mess about at the back or put himself under pressure, which is the sort of centre-back I like.

JACK CHARLTON

David O'Leary was a 1980 version of Virgil van Dijk – a Rolls-Royce of a defender.

JOHN DEVINE

For a lad coming over from Dublin at 15 to say you'd be at Arsenal for 20 years, you'd play the most games and all that, you look at that and think: 'Good God, I got very lucky really.'

DAVID O'LEARY

I knew we were in a good team, but it was a special, special night [when Arsenal won the league in 1989]. Michael Thomas, the goal he scored, my brother and my dad were behind that goal. It was fantastic when we won it to see them there afterwards. It was a very special night in a very special ground against a very special club.

DAVID O'LEARY

Sol Campbell
2001 – 2006 and 2010

Following the rarely trodden path that few would even consider, Sol Campbell moved from Tottenham Hotspur to join Arsenal. Considered a Spurs legend, the move infuriated their supporters and it's fair to say some of them never let him forget what they saw as the most heinous transfer possible.

The Gunners were delighted: not only were they signing one of the Premier League's best centre-backs and a seasoned England international – he also arrived on a free transfer. Campbell undoubtedly improved at Arsenal, where he took his game to the next level and began winning trophies. A defensive rock and genuine athlete, few got the better of him, and his five-year stay – plus a brief return four years later in 2010 – could not have gone much better.

GAMES and GOALS

League	146	8
FA Cup	20	2
League Cup	2	0
Europe	41	2
Other	2	0
Total	**211**	**12**

TROPHIES

Premier League x 2
FA Cup x 2
FA Community Shield x 1

We're better when Sol's at the back...
When you have Sol at the back it gives you the
confidence you need.

THIERRY HENRY

Sol has been a giant for us... the younger players,
who have progressed here over recent times,
have benefited hugely from playing alongside Sol.

ARSÈNE WENGER

I'm a street footballer. I'm hardcore. Growing up in east London, you've got to be a little bit self-confident. As a player, I would go into detail, watch who I was playing against. Who might come into my vicinity. That gives you self-confidence.

SOL CAMPBELL

Playing for Arsenal was not just a career choice; it was a commitment to excellence.

SOL CAMPBELL

Lee Dixon
1988 – 2002

A right-back who would become the fourth-highest appearance maker for the Gunners, Lee Dixon was an almost permanent fixture in the Arsenal starting XI for almost 14 years.

Signed from Stoke City in 1988, the Manchester-born defender was a model of commitment and consistency. Dixon was an intelligent full-back who enjoyed supporting attacks – as a healthy assist and goals record proves. Dixon was forced to almost reinvent himself with the arrival of Arsène Wenger, but he adapted to a more attacking style well and proved a valuable first team member all the way up to his 14th and final season.

GAMES and GOALS

League	458	24
FA Cup	54	1
League Cup	43	0
Europe	58	2
Other	3	0
Total	**616**	**27**

TROPHIES

First Division/Premier League x 4

FA Cup x 3

FA Charity/Community Shield x 3

European Cup Winners' Cup x 1

We've had an offer from Arsenal. We're not standing in your way, it's good for the club and it's good for you.

MICK MILLS
then Stoke manager

Lee Dixon's strengths are different [from Nigel Winterburn]. He is very competent defensively, but he likes to get forward. Arsenal have not used traditional wingers on the right because he gives them that option.

BRIAN MARWOOD

I was fortunate to play in an Arsenal back line that earned itself a reputation as being OK. I'm not trying to be overly modest in saying that, as individuals, we weren't the best players in the world. But certainly all my weaknesses were compensated for by Tony Adams, Nigel Winterburn, Martin Keown and Steve Bould, and vice versa. If one of us wasn't playing well, the others picked up the slack.

LEE DIXON

I've never been a goalscorer, only own goals. Good own goals.

LEE DIXON

Pat Rice

1967 – 1980

Arsenal's right-back for a decade and with more than 500 appearances under his belt, Pat Rice was a model of consistency and reliability during his 13 years at Highbury. The Northern Ireland international came through the youth ranks but had to wait for his opportunity in the first team, playing just a handful of games in his first three seasons. Once he had established himself, however, Rice became almost an immovable object.

He was handed the captaincy for the final three years of his time with the Gunners , leading the team out at Wembley for three successive FA Cup finals – though only one would result in victory. Rice would appear in five FA Cup finals for the Gunners during his long, distinguished career in North London.

GAMES and GOALS

League	396	11
FA Cup	35	0
League Cup	11	0
Europe	27	0
Other	1	0
Total	**470**	**11**

TROPHIES

First Division x 1

FA Cup x 2

Pat is the ultimate loyal servant to Arsenal. It is in his DNA. He is the one the club always put up as an example. They'd say: 'If you want to make it, this is the guy to emulate.' He was a great captain, inspiring. He'd remind us it was never over until it was over.

LIAM BRADY

Mr Pat Rice... 44 years at the Arsenal... Take a bow! Thanks for everything you have done for me.

JACK WILSHERE

on Twitter/X

The spirit of the side was remarkable, much as it is now with the current squad. But I think it meant just a bit more to the players like Frank McLintock, George Armstrong and George Graham, the older ones who had been through it all for years trying to get the title back to Arsenal.

PAT RICE

Now it was our turn. Yes, we celebrated for a good while – ironically enough, at a pub called the White Hart!

PAT RICE

recalling the celebrations after a 2–2 draw at White Hart Lane secured the First Division Championship

Ashley Cole
1999 – 2006

A product of the Arsenal youth system, Ashley Cole would grow to become one of the best left-backs in world football. Cole was an attack-minded defender who slotted perfectly into Arsène Wenger's masterplan and was a determined, focused and studious footballer, always looking to improve himself and learn from the best.

He would play in the first team for the best part of seven seasons, and though he would leave the club in controversial circumstances, when he was wearing a red and white shirt, he gave excellent service.

GAMES and GOALS

League 156 8
FA Cup 20 0
League Cup 3 0
Europe 45 1
Other 4 0
Total .... **228** **9**

TROPHIES

Premier League x 3
FA Cup x 3
FA Charity/Community Shield x 2

He is a defender who simply loves to attack.
Defends because he has to defend and because it
is part of his job. Everybody loves to play with
[him] because as soon as you won the ball back,
he was up there to attack.

ARSÈNE WENGER

After Sylvinho you [Cole] can play left-back.
You are one of the best left-backs at the club and
one day will be one of the best in the world.

ARSÈNE WENGER

Roberto Carlos has got natural talent, but I think if you train hard enough you can be nearly as good as that.

ASHLEY COLE

I'd love to be captain of Arsenal for even just one day.

ASHLEY COLE

Frank McLintock

1964 – 1973

Gritty Scot Frank McLintock was no overnight success at Highbury, taking the best part of five years – and a change in position – to really find his feet at Arsenal.

Initially brought in as a right-half, manager Bertie Mee recognised McLintock had leadership skills and ability that was better suited in the centre of defence. Once the switch was made, McLintock went from strength to strength, became captain of the team and led the Gunners to European glory in the Inter-Cities Fairs Cup and then the 1970–71 Double. He gave nine years of excellent service and is remembered as one of the club's greatest captains.

GAMES and GOALS

League	314	26
FA Cup	36	1
League Cup	34	4
Europe	19	1
Other	0	0
Total	**403**	**32**

TROPHIES

First Division x 1

FA Cup x 1

Inter-Cities Fairs Cup x 1

Did you know?

To rid the team of expectation and comparison to past great teams of Arsenal's past, McLintock insisted the team change their strip to all red for the 1966–67 season.

The change lasted just one season before reverting to the traditional red and white of today.

It meant everything to win that league, and then the cup. It was my pinnacle. It was our pinnacle as a team.

FRANK McLINTOCK

The Fairs Cup win in 1970 was a turning point in my life. Beating Anderlecht was beautiful. I was a winner. Arsenal were winners.

FRANK McLINTOCK

CHAPTER
3

THE GREATEST MIDFIELDERS

Arsenal fans love nothing more than a skilful playmaker, able to mix artistry with industry and create memorable moments. Here are some of the best to patrol the middle of the park for the Gunners...

Patrick Vieira
1996 – 2005

It's hard to imagine a more influential midfielder than Patrick Vieira. A natural leader on and off the pitch, Vieira had a little bit of everything and it's no coincidence that his time with the Gunners was also one of the club's most successful periods.

A relative unknown when he joined from AC Milan in 1996, Vieira would be pivotal in new manager Arsène Wenger's plans. The French boss would build his team around the imposing No. 4 who would go on to become one of the greatest players the Premier League has ever seen.

The driving force behind one of the greatest Arsenal teams of any era, Vieira was a class act with an edge!

GAMES and GOALS

League	279	29
FA Cup	48	3
League Cup	11	0
Europe	68	2
Other	3	0
Total	**409**	**34**

TROPHIES

Premier League x 3

FA Cup x 4

FA Charity/Community Shield x 3

Two players in one. He has tremendous physique, but also sophisticated technique. And what is very important for a modern midfielder, he has the goalscorer's instinct.

MARCEL DESAILLY

We both had that winners' mindset... If anyone knew that, it was Patrick Vieira. He's the type who gives 100 percent in every situation, and I saw how he boosted the entire team. There aren't many football players I have that kind of respect for.

ZLATAN IBRAHIMOVIĆ

My commitment, and my desire to win the ball or make a tackle, that will never change. But you grow up. I'm not 20 anymore.

PATRICK VIEIRA

I didn't know anything about England or anything about Arsenal, but I knew a lot about Arsène and his reputation, so I went straight away.

PATRICK VIEIRA

Marc Overmars
1997 – 2000

Marc Overmars had established himself as one of Europe's most exciting young talents while with Ajax, but a serious knee injury meant Arsenal's decision to sign the Dutchman was something of a risk. But if that had been a gamble, it soon proved to be a fantastic piece of business, as Overmars settled into Premier League life like the proverbial duck to water. Fast, dynamic and intelligent, Overmars became one of the English game's most feared wingers, with the ability to give any full-back a miserable afternoon.

He was a constant fixture of Arsène Wenger's team for the three seasons he played for the Gunners, winning an army of admirers in the process before he left for Barcelona. An exciting talent.

GAMES and GOALS

League	100	25
FA Cup	16	6
League Cup	5	2
Europe	20	6
Other	1	1
Total	**142**	**40**

TROPHIES

Premier League x 1
FA Cup x 1
FA Charity Shield x 1

All Europe thought Overmars was dead because of his damaged knee, but in every important game we have had this season, he has scored.

ARSÈNE WENGER

Marc has great mental strength. He is a world-class player.

ARSÈNE WENGER

I like English football because there is more pace. With my speed and quality I think it will be good for me here.

MARC OVERMARS

I enjoyed my time at Arsenal unbelievably. The atmosphere was good of course – in the stadium and in the dressing room – and it was a great period for the club. I had three years of success there and from a personal point of view, they were the best years of my career.

MARC OVERMARS

Martin Ødegaard

2021 – present day

Martin Ødegaard was a teenage wonderkid who moved to Real Madrid. A series of loan moves followed until Mikel Arteta brought him to the Emirates – also on loan – in January 2021. Finally, the talented Norwegian began to shine, and the Gunners made the deal permanent the following August for a fee in the region of £30 million.

It would prove an absolute steal. Ødegaard's nomadic existence was over, he had found his home and the promise he'd shown as a teen in Norway began to blossom. Since then Ødegaard has become the beating heart of Arsenal, taken on the captaincy and is among the very best midfielders in the world.

GAMES and GOALS*

League	137	32
FA Cup	4	0
League Cup	7	1
Europe	27	4
Other	1	0
Total	**176**	**37**

as of 31/01/2025

TROPHIES

FA Community Shield x 1

Martin Ødegaard is in a different class, what a player. He makes Bukayo Saka 10 times better! Don't get me wrong, Saka is a good player, but Ødegaard just elevates him to another level.

PAUL MERSON

I think he's one of the best midfielders in the world. We are better with him and he's top three [in the world]. I don't want to put too much pressure on him but I think top three. I love this guy.

WILLIAM SALIBA

My story has been a bit different. I moved when I was 16 and then changed teams here and there on loan, so for me it's been a key thing to find a place where I could really settle down. I've felt at home here since the first day; I just felt great. This is definitely my home and I'm so happy to be here.

MARTIN ØDEGAARD

I enjoy a little pressure that you have to perform, and people expect you to do well; I think it's a good thing. But it's important to stay focused on the right things. For us, the main thing is just to focus on how we can improve as a team, take new steps all the time, and push each other every day in training.

MARTIN ØDEGAARD

Liam Brady

1973 – 1980

From 1973 to 1980, Liam Brady graced Arsenal's midfield with the sort of vision and skill rarely seen in the English top flight. Brady was a gifted playmaker with a left foot capable of magical things.

Brady glided around the pitch with grace and poise and soon progressed to be a Highbury terrace idol. He was the sort of player coveted by other clubs at home and abroad. He pretty much had it all, with the ability to create and score spectacular goals, but the lure of playing in Europe eventually proved too great for the Irishman and he left for Juventus in 1980, where he was handed the coveted No. 10 shirt. A class act.

GAMES and GOALS

League	235	43
FA Cup	20	2
League Cup	7	3
Europe	13	4
Other	1	0
Total	**276**	**52**

TROPHIES

FA Cup x 1

Liam was the best player I ever played with. That burst of acceleration he had, it took him away from people, always leaving you with the impression he had space on the ball. I don't care what anyone says – Liam was as good as Michel Platini, as talented as any player in the world.

JOHN DEVINE

Look at that! Oh look at that! What a goal by Brady!

JOHN MOTSON

When I look back from this distance, there's a little bit of regret that I didn't push myself harder. With more dedication, I could have been a lot better with my right foot and a lot stronger physically. It was complacency, to some extent. I knew I had more ability than my team-mates in the youths.

LIAM BRADY

[Italy] was easy, compared to the rough and tumble of English football and how hard it was. Italy was a doddle compared to playing against Liverpool and the likes of Jimmy Case and Tommy Smith.

LIAM BRADY

Emmanuel Petit

1997 – 2000

For three years, Emmanuel Petit formed one of European football's most formidable partnerships alongside Patrick Vieira, where their understanding, power and nous made Arsenal such a powerhouse in the 1990s and early 2000s.

Like Vieira, little was known of Petit on these shores when he signed from Monaco, but the tall, long-haired Frenchman was soon a crowd favourite at Highbury. Petit would chip in with some important goals, too. Arsène Wenger converted him from a central defender to holding midfielder and the Double was secured in his first campaign. He left after three seasons to join Barcelona.

GAMES and GOALS

League	85	9
FA Cup	13	2
League Cup	3	0
Europe	15	0
Other	2	0
Total	**118**	**11**

TROPHIES

Premier League x 1

FA Cup x 1

FA Charity Shield x 2

He is a player who will give 100 per cent
and somebody who never lets his friends down.

FRANK LEBOEUF

He was the perfect player for me at that time,
because with his quality, I think we were quite
really good together.

PATRICK VIEIRA

I always loved Barcelona and [Real] Madrid, two of the biggest clubs in the world. But I should have stayed with Arsenal, definitely.

EMMANUEL PETIT

You know, sometimes the grass is not greener somewhere else. It's better to stay where you are when you receive love and happiness, and you are successful. Why would you leave? Leaving Arsenal is definitely a big regret. If I could turn the clock back, I would probably make a different decision.

EMMANUEL PETIT

David Rocastle
1985 – 1992

You'd be hard-pressed to find a more popular or likeable player than David Rocastle, who graced Arsenal's first team for six seasons. A huge fan favourite, "Rocky" came through the club's youth ranks before establishing himself in the first team.

A bundle of energy and invention, Rocastle could provide the spark of magic in tight games, either with a goal or spectacular pass. He was a joy to watch and very much one of the Arsenal fans' "own", clocking up 276 appearances along the way. He was surprisingly sold to Leeds United and later played for Manchester City, but Rocky – who tragically died aged only 33 – enjoyed his best years as a Gunner.

GAMES and GOALS

League	218	24
FA Cup	20	4
League Cup	33	6
Europe	4	0
Other	1	0
Total	**276**	**34**

TROPHIES

First Division x 2
League Cup x 1
FA Charity Shield x 1

He was a really top talent who had just about everything – he had all-round ability.

FRANK McLINTOCK

You know what? Billy Joel sings that song 'Only The Good Die Young'. And that is him.

PAUL MERSON

Remember who you are, what you are and who you represent.

DAVID ROCASTLE

Whatever happens in life from now on, no one will be able to take away what I achieved. You can't live in the past while you're still playing but after you've finished no one will be able to take away the fact that I played that night at Anfield in '89.

DAVID ROCASTLE

Ray Parlour

1992 – 2004

Ray Parlour spent almost two decades with Arsenal as man and boy, becoming one of the club's greatest servants in the process. The perfect example of a player who worked tirelessly for the cause, rather than his own personal profile, the curly-haired midfielder – nicknamed "The Romford Pele" by supporters – cut a dashing figure as he patrolled Highbury.

Tenacious and industrious, Parlour's technique and all-round game improved as he got older, with the likes of Patrick Vieira and Dennis Bergkamp to learn off. His 13 seasons in the first team yielded numerous trophies and were just reward for this often underrated Arsenal star.

GAMES and GOALS

League	339	22
FA Cup	44	4
League Cup	26	0
Europe	58	6
Other	4	0
Total	**471**	**32**

TROPHIES

Premier League x 3

FA Cup x 4

League Cup x 1

FA Charity/Community Shield x 3

European Cup Winners' Cup x 1

What a player this kid Cesc Fàbregas is, boss!

RAY PARLOUR

Yes, Ray, he's taking your position!

ARSÈNE WENGER

Sometimes you can't be as good as Dennis Bergkamp or Thierry Henry, but you have to be similar. That's what Arsène Wenger had. The will to win was unbelievable in that team.

RAY PARLOUR

We never knew when we were beaten. The best example was we did these eight against eights we'd do at training on a Friday before a Saturday game. We'd do a game like that with the eleven players starting and the five subs. The lads were really putting in tackles and going for it. No one wanted to lose that. Wenger sometimes said, 'Lads we've got a big game tomorrow, don't injure yourselves.' It was tough.

RAY PARLOUR

Cesc Fàbregas

2003 – 2011

With limited senior opportunities at his boyhood club Barcelona, Cesc Fàbregas, a 16-year-old Catalan, took the opportunity to move to London and try his luck at Arsenal. It would prove a wise career move for the talented midfield playmaker. He became the club's youngest debutant and goalscorer and quickly gained a reputation as one of the best young midfielders in Europe.

From 2004 to 2011, Fàbregas, who bravely took on the No. 4 shirt – and void – left by Patrick Vieira, would rarely miss a game, with his average of a goal every six games a more than decent return. A classy footballer who created countless opportunities for his team-mates, Fàbregas was a modern, intelligent and fine servant for the Gunners.

GAMES and GOALS

League	212	35
FA Cup	14	2
League Cup	14	2
Europe	61	17
Other	2	1
Total	**303**	**57**

TROPHIES

FA Cup x 1

FA Community Shield x 1

The player who has created so much excitement and generated so much interest, even more so than [José Antonio] Reyes, is the young boy Fàbregas. He is another diamond that Arsène Wenger has unearthed. From everything I've seen and everything I've heard about him, it is clear that Fàbregas is going to be an absolutely massive, massive star player. I think Fàbregas is one of the best young players there has ever been.

BOB WILSON

It is not stupid to think that he could be called up for the Spain first team. They have a lot of midfielders in Spain at the moment, but they should not be scared to take him. He has been consistent, his work-rate and commitment are outstanding, and his football is a joy to watch.

ARSÈNE WENGER

I certainly wasn't thinking about it. I knew they were great players, but I also never really thought of the first team at that point. I mean, I was there to play for the youth team, I never imagined I would have to worry about the first team's midfield. I was 16 years old... normally players get a chance when they turn 22 or thereabouts. I thought it would be the same for me. I certainly did not imagine that, in less than a year, I'd be playing regularly alongside them.

CESC FÀBREGAS

Vieira said that what mattered was giving 100 per cent, knowing that you might not get 100 per cent back from your performance. His words had a massive impact on me, not least because he was my captain and a guy who played in my position on the pitch.

CESC FÀBREGAS

CHAPTER
4

THE GREATEST FORWARDS

Arsenal can boast a plethora of great
wingers and strikers over the years –
some of the game's true greats – most
of whom shone brightest in the red
and white of the Gunners...

Cliff Bastin

1929 – 1947

Though Cliff Bastin and his wonderful exploits in the past might have been a name largely confined to the history books, the pursuit of his record goal-scoring feats were deservedly highlighted again by Ian Wright's pursuit of his No. 1 spot.

Bastin's goal haul of 178 was a record that stood from 1939 to 1997 before Ian Wright eventually surpassed it and, in turn, Thierry Henry took the mantle. One can only imagine how many goals Bastin, part of an all-conquering Gunners team of the early 1930s, might have ended up with but for the six-year suspension of league football due to the Second World War at a time when the 27-year-old Bastin was at the peak of his powers.

GAMES and GOALS

League	350	150
FA Cup	42	26
League Cup	0	0
Europe	0	0
Other	4	2
Total	**396**	**178**

TROPHIES

First Division x 5

FA Cup x 2

FA Charity Shield x 3

Did you know?

Cliff Bastin appeared in two wartime movies – *The Arsenal Stadium Mystery* in 1939, which included shots of the last game at Highbury before the outbreak of the Second World War, and then in 1942 he played a footballer in the classic British war film *One of Our Aircraft is Missing*.

This Arsenal team of 1930–31 was the finest eleven I ever played in. And, without hesitation, I include in that generalisation international teams as well. Never before had there been such a team put out by any club – and never since have I seen it rivalled.

CLIFF BASTIN

Coupled with his sincerity and his loyalty to all his bosses, he had a trait few of us are blessed with – that is, an ice-cold temperament.

TOM WHITTAKER

Ian Wright

1991 – 1998

A striker who was the very embodiment of Arsenal Football Club, Ian Wright was born to be a Gunner. It's not often in football you get a perfect fit of player and club, but Wright achieved legendary status at Highbury during a stunning seven-year stay – his mixture of energy, industry, skill and goalscoring made him one of the best in Europe.

A scorer of every type of goal, "Wrighty" was just as likely to send a 25-yarder in the top corner as he was to tap in at the far post. Rightly adored by the fans, he forever wrote his name in the history books when he finally broke Cliff Bastin's club record as the all-time top goal-scorer. Impudent, mischievous and colourful, Ian Wright was all that and more.

GAMES and GOALS

League	221	128
FA Cup	16	12
League Cup	29	29
Europe	19	15
Other	3	1
Total	**288**	**185**

TROPHIES

Premier League x 1

FA Cup x 2

League Cup x 1

European Cup Winners' Cup x 1

Ian is a very infectious character who
contributed a great deal to the dressing room
and did his very best when on the pitch.

KENNY DALGLISH

Ian lit up the pitch and dressing room with the
electricity of his performances and his personality.

GEORGE GRAHAM

I have so many fantastic memories at Highbury, but I don't visit very often because the place is obviously very different now – it is flats and gardens, not the football stadium I loved to play and score at.

I am so pleased that it was the setting for one of the proudest moments of my career, when I broke Cliff Bastin's goalscoring record.

For me to have done that, to have been the greatest goalscorer in Arsenal's history, is still difficult for me to comprehend even when people tell me they were there to see it happen – which a lot of people do.

IAN WRIGHT

Dennis Bergkamp
1995 – 2006

Dennis Bergkamp was 26 years old and already had more than 300 appearances under his belt when he joined Arsenal from Inter Milan in 1995. The £7.5 million fee was hardly a gamble, but few could have realised the impact the elegant Dutch forward would have at Highbury. Schooled by the Ajax ethos of Total Football, Bergkamp soon captivated not only the Arsenal fans, but the rest of English football and far beyond these shores.

Not a striker and not an attacking midfielder, Bergkamp almost invented a role that was hard to describe, and he created and scored some of the most beautiful goals the club had ever seen. A joy to watch, he is undoubtedly one of the greatest footballers ever to play for Arsenal.

GAMES and GOALS

League	315	87
FA Cup	39	14
League Cup	16	8
Europe	48	11
Other	5	0
Total	**423**	**120**

TROPHIES

Premier League x 3
FA Cup x 3
FA Charity/Community Shield x 3

Dennis was a dream for a striker.

THIERRY HENRY

You can't blame anyone for that. You just have to accept that Bergkamp did a beautiful thing.

SIR BOBBY ROBSON

on Bergkamp's goal v Newcastle, March 2002

I think these awards are always nice for a player, but they also reflect well on the club. It shows that Arsenal's performance has been noted all around the world and it helps by having so many good players around me.

DENNIS BERGKAMP

Other clubs never came into my thoughts once I knew Arsenal wanted to sign me.

DENNIS BERGKAMP

Bukayo Saka

2018 – present day

Bukayo Saka joined Arsenal at the age of seven and steadily moved through the youth ranks to become one of the club's most exciting home grown talents. A dynamic, fast and skilful right winger, Saka broke into the first team during the 2019–20 season and has rarely been out of it since.

Spearheading a new era for the Gunners, Saka is the poster boy at the Emirates Stadium and represents the attack-minded football the club has become synonymous with during their Premier League title quest. A scorer and creator of wonderful goals, Saka is already well on his way to becoming a modern day Arsenal legend.

GAMES and GOALS*

League	186	52
FA Cup	11	1
League Cup	12	1
Europe	39	13
Other	2	0
Total	**250**	**67**

as of 31/01/2025

TROPHIES

FA Cup x 1

FA Community Shield x 2

If there's a better player in world football at the moment, someone who both scores and makes goals, the only one I can think of is Lionel Messi.

TONY ADAMS

I can't talk highly enough of the lad. He's improved immensely and I don't mean improved because he now goes past four or five players, but it's his end product. He's got a great calmness about him. He's only 21, there's plenty more to come from him. He won't play his best football until he's 26, 27 or 28.

PAUL MERSON

I've always dreamed of this moment from when I was a kid to score a goal for Arsenal Football Club.

BUKAYO SAKA

I was standing on the pitch at Old Trafford before the game. It was just my second-ever start in the Premier League – and it finally hit me: I'm in the Arsenal first team.

BUKAYO SAKA

Malcolm Macdonald

1976 – 1979

The signing of prolific Newcastle United striker Malcolm Macdonald in 1976 was arguably one of the Gunners' most exciting transfer deals up to that point. "Supermac" was idolised on Tyneside where he had achieved legendary status by scoring 138 goals in 257 appearances.

A Londoner, Macdonald was an instant hit at Highbury, top scoring in his first two seasons before sustaining a serious knee injury that would all but end his career aged 29. How many more goals Supermac would have scored for the Gunners one can only guess, but his 57 strikes in 108 starts suggests it would have been a sizeable haul.

GAMES and GOALS

League	84	42
FA Cup	9	10
League Cup	14	5
Europe	0	0
Other	1	0
Total	**108**	**57**

TROPHIES

None

Supermac, superstar, how many goals
have you scored so far?

ARSENAL FAN CHANT

He lived on goals – he thrived on scoring goals.

ALAN BALL

I taught myself to put them into the top corner – hit them so hard that the goalie could not do anything about it. We never lost on penalties.

MALCOLM MACDONALD

You do your job, I'll do mine – that's putting the ball in the back of the net.

MALCOLM MACDONALD

Thierry Henry
1999 – 2007 and 2012

Regarded as the best player ever to pull on an Arsenal shirt, Thierry Henry's legacy with the Gunners will continue for many years and his name will never be forgotten. Etched into the history books as the Gunners' all-time top goal-scorer, Henry was a wonderful footballer to watch.

Blessed with electric pace, he could score any type of goal but, more often than not, it would be something pretty spectacular. Henry could do it all – score, create for team-mates, take penalties and free-kicks as well as wearing the captain's armband. And he wasn't just a Gunners great, he was a world superstar who, for eight years, strutted his stuff in North London when Arsène Wenger's team were at their very peak. An incredible talent.

GAMES and GOALS

League	258	175
FA Cup	26	8
League Cup	3	2
Europe	86	42
Other	4	1
Total	**377**	**228**

TROPHIES

Premier League x 2
FA Cup x 2
FA Community Shield x 2

He's probably been the finest player Arsenal have ever had so you can't dismiss five or six great seasons that he gave us. I think the fans should leave with a warm feeling for Thierry Henry. He deserves it – he has been magnificent.

FRANK McLINTOCK

He was one of the greatest players I've ever seen, and I've seen a few good ones.

ARSÈNE WENGER

But I will miss the Arsenal fans dearly, they have supported me through thick and thin. They will always be in my heart, as will all the fans who make the game here so special. I will always have a special bond with Arsenal Football Club.

THIERRY HENRY

I always said I was never going to come back and play in Europe again but, when the team you love and support asks you back, it's kind of hard to say 'no'.

THIERRY HENRY

on his return to the club in 2012

Robin van Persie

2004 – 2012

Arsenal's habit of unearthing Dutch gems continued when Robin van Persie joined the club from Feyenoord in 2004.

A classy striker capable of the incredible and simplistic, Van Persie quickly became a Gunners favourite with his goal-scoring feats. He reached double figures in all but one of his eight seasons in North London and seemed to improve with age. Indeed, his final season at the Emirates saw him bag a fantastic 37 goals in just 42 games – that would attract the interest of Manchester United and the Dutch star headed north – but his service in the red and white of Arsenal saw him finish as one of the club's top 10 goal-scorers of all time.

GAMES and GOALS

League	194	96
FA Cup	18	10
League Cup	11	6
Europe	53	20
Other	2	0
Total	**278**	**132**

TROPHIES

FA Cup x 1

FA Community Shield x 1

Van Persie is the complete player. He has the entire package. He is a good footballer, but he scores loads of goals at the same time.

LIONEL MESSI

It was outstanding, quite unbelievable. Nobody expected that. When Eboue crossed I did not see anybody in the box, so I thought, like many times, we have nobody in there. Then suddenly Van Persie arrives. Technically it was perfect, with full pace and power. I felt the ball would go over the bar at the start, then it finished in the top corner. It is the goal of a lifetime.

ARSÈNE WENGER
on RVP's goal v Charlton 2006

It's my dream and I see no point in speaking about other teams when I have these dreams. I think other people know that about me; I'm just hungry to win with Arsenal and that's it.

ROBIN VAN PERSIE

Every big player who leaves Arsenal is a massive loss. But no player here is bigger than the club.

ROBIN VAN PERSIE

John Radford
1964 – 1976

For 14 years, forward John Radford gave everything for Arsenal. The gritty, hard-working Yorkshireman might not be spoken about in the same revered tones as Ian Wright, Cliff Bastin or Thierry Henry, but his contribution, games played, and goals return are all up there with the best of them.

Radford was happy to stay in the background, always working hard for the team over personal glory. Steadily, his stats grew, the goals kept going in and his tally of 149 is the fourth best in Arsenal history.

GAMES and GOALS

League 379 111
FA Cup 44 15
League Cup 34 12
Europe 24 11
Other......................... 0 0
Total .... **481** **149**

TROPHIES

First Division x 1
FA Cup x 1

Inter-City Fairs Cup x 1

Did you know?

In the 1971–72 season Arsenal keeper Bob Wilson was forced to go off injured against Stoke in the FA Cup semi-final. Radford went in goal and Arsenal secured a 1–1 draw – to round things off, Radford then scored the winning goal in the replay as Arsenal again progressed to the final.

Bob Wilson was injured late in the second half and I took over for the last 15 minutes. They couldn't get one past me that day and I loved every minute of it!

JOHN RADFORD

That's my best memory, even more than doing the Double, because it was the club's first trophy for 17 years.

JOHN RADFORD

on scoring in the 1970 Fairs Cup second leg

Charlie Nicholas

1983 – 1988

Charlie Nicholas arrived in North London as a Celtic superstar. North of the Border, Nicholas had scored 47 goals in 53 games for Celtic and, understandably, the capture of Scotland's brightest talent caused a great deal of excitement among Gunners fans. Nicholas was blessed with wonderful technical ability and skill – he was an entertainer that football fans adored around the nation, and he was soon strutting his stuff at Highbury.

Nicknamed "Champagne Charlie", the bright lights of London probably didn't enhance his career and he would stay just four seasons – but the fact he is still talked of in revered terms several decades later is testament to his popularity.

GAMES and GOALS

League	151	34
FA Cup	13	10
League Cup	20	10
Europe	0	0
Other	0	0
Total	**184**	**54**

TROPHIES

League Cup x 1

In the best traditions of Scottish football, Peter Marinello and Charlie loved to entertain crowds and dazzle with their footwork, but in order to be successful, and to play in a winning team, a player needs focus and discipline.

GEORGE GRAHAM

You are wasting your talent.

GEORGE GRAHAM

"

What does Arsenal mean? It means class. The structure of the club, everything has a classy feel about it. It isn't always about success, there is more than that and this is what makes it a cut above the rest.

"

CHARLIE NICHOLAS

"

I got the reputation of earring and no socks. In those days we were open with the press boys because they trusted us. We could go for a drink with them, whereas now everything is scrutinised. At that time there was Frank McAvennie and Mo Johnston. We were all a bit maverick. The only harm we ever did was probably to ourselves, our own reputation.

"

CHARLIE NICHOLAS

Charlie George
1968 – 1975

Local lad made good, Charlie George was the kid who watched Arsenal from the terraces and then went on to play for his heroes – and he loved every minute of it. George had the looks and personality of a rock star and cut a dashing figure on the pitch, where he loved nothing more than entertaining the fans and giving his all for the club.

His stats may not measure up against some of the other Arsenal legends, but his popularity puts him up there with the very best. His goal against Liverpool in the 1971 FA Cup final secured the Double and his celebration – lying on his back with his arms in the air – is probably the most iconic image in the club's history.

GAMES and GOALS

League	133	31
FA Cup	22	11
League Cup	8	2
Europe	16	5
Other	0	0
Total	**179**	**49**

TROPHIES

First Division x 1

FA Cup x 1

Inter-Cities Fairs Cup x 1

What should be remembered is that this boy is just 20 years old and that a bit of devilment is part and parcel of the game.

ALAN BALL

Get your hair cut, get your hair cut, get your hair cut, Charlie George!

OPPOSITION SUPPORTERS' CHANT

I played football with me head, not my hair.

CHARLIE GEORGE

I fell down because I didn't have another drop of energy left in me. I wasn't thinking that I ought to do something that people will remember. I was just f***ing knackered.

CHARLIE GEORGE

on that 1971 FA Cup final celebration, after scoring the winning goal in extra time that secured Arsenal's first Double

Robert Pires

2000 – 2006

Wearing David Rocastle's No. 7 shirt and brought in as a replacement for Marc Overmars, the weight and expectation on new signing Robert Pires' shoulders was huge – not that anyone would have ever guessed. He took time to settle into life at Arsenal, but once he had, there was no stopping Pires, who was blessed with the vision and technique of a world-class playmaker and the finishing of a top striker.

Along with Ashley Cole and Thierry Henry, the trio gave the Gunners a left-sided threat that led to trophy after trophy. For six seasons, Pires was superb and a vital cog in Arsène Wenger's all-conquering side.

GAMES and GOALS

League	189	62
FA Cup	28	10
League Cup	2	1
Europe	63	11
Other	2	0
Total	**284**	**84**

TROPHIES

Premier League x 2

FA Cup x 2

He will gain respect. But I am sure Robert Pires isn't coming here just to be a player that everyone is going to stand back and admire... He will want to gain the respect... he is a fantastic trainer... he loves to practise, he loves to play.

ARSÈNE WENGER

We knew Robert had talent, but the Premiership has made him take on a new dimension... Robert has shown proof of his intelligence. Technically, he was always there, but his game has become more direct. You feel that he has become liberated on and off the pitch. He is giving everything he has... When you have technique like his, you know you can come out of things well anywhere on the field.

THIERRY HENRY

When I think of Arsenal, my favourite personal memory that I recall is scoring my first goal for the club – away to Lazio in the Champions League. It was important because when you join a new club, you really want to score your first goal. It's where everything started for me at this club.

ROBERT PIRES

In England, football is a religion. In France, football is not a religion. It's wine and food.

ROBERT PIRES

Paul Merson

1984 – 1997

For mearly 15 years, Paul Merson and Arsenal were almost inseparable. The young Londoner joined the club as an apprentice and worked his way into the first team where he would quickly become a permanent fixture. Though he began life as a striker, "Merse" was soon utilised as a deep-lying forward or playmaker, where his talent shone through. Merson was capable of wonderful goals and passes and had that sprinkling of magic dust that made him stand out.

Loved by the Arsenal fans, he had to battle his way through a difficult period of his life when addictions were badly affecting his form, but he fought through them and remains a firm fan favourite to this day.

GAMES and GOALS

League	327	78
FA Cup	27	4
League Cup	36	10
Europe	21	7
Other	6	0
Total	**417**	**99**

TROPHIES

First Division x 2

FA Cup x 2

League Cup x 1

FA Charity Shield x 1

European Cup Winners' Cup x 1

Did you know?

Merson, a lifelong Chelsea fan, has released several bestselling books since his retirement as a player and is one of Sky Sports' longest-serving pundits, loved by Arsenal fans for his bubbly, down-to-earth character.

Arsenal is a Rolls-Royce of a club. A truly great club. Everything was perfect at Arsenal. You don't fully appreciate how special the club is until you leave, to be honest, because you are spoiled at the club, and it becomes the norm to you.

PAUL MERSON

I played for some special clubs after Arsenal, but nothing will top Arsenal. The club was incredible from top to bottom.

PAUL MERSON

Freddie Ljungberg

1998 – 2007

For eight fantastic seasons, Freddie Ljungberg thrilled Arsenal fans. From the moment he scored against Manchester United just moments into his debut, the Swedish attacking midfielder never looked back and forged a wonderful understanding with Dennis Bergkamp and Robert Pires as Arsène Wenger's side dominated domestic football for several years.

Ljungberg was a tireless and dynamic worker, scoring many vital goals and creating many others. He became a huge favourite during his time with the Gunners and could play anywhere in the middle, or on the flanks when needed, with only injuries hampering his later years with the club.

GAMES and GOALS

League	216	46
FA Cup	32	11
League Cup	3	0
Europe	73	15
Other	1	0
Total	**325**	**72**

TROPHIES

Premier League x 2

FA Cup x 3

FA Charity Shield x 1

"

I always thought a big part of Freddie's game as a player was his brain and his ability to pick the right options. When you play like he did, you have got to be intelligent. You have got to know the game, know what defenders are thinking. He was not reacting on instinct. He could work out where the gaps were going to be and the timing of the run needed.

"

LEE DIXON

"

The vainest? I think it's Freddie Ljungberg. Yeah, because his best friend was the mirror. Before the game his preparation was fantastic. Freddie was a great player, but he was also the model. So that's why. So yeah, the most vain player was Freddie Ljungberg!

"

RAY PARLOUR

The important thing for me is we want to keep the ball; we want to have the ball because we are Arsenal football club.

FREDDIE LJUNGBERG

If you want to play at Arsenal you need to be top, top, you need precision.

FREDDIE LJUNGBERG

Nwankwo Kanu
1999 – 2004

Some players are born to play for Arsenal – and Nigerian forward Kanu was one of them. There was a joy to Kanu's game that was infectious – his languid style initially didn't ignite with Gunners fans, but he had magic in his boots and he quickly became a cult figure at the club.

Kanu was capable of impossible goals and devastating passages of play when he could destroy teams, but he was also loved because there was a joy to his game and his infectious smile and enthusiasm made him a player fans still talk fondly of to the present day.

GAMES and GOALS

League	119	30
FA Cup	17	3
League Cup	8	4
Europe	53	6
Other	1	1
Total	**198**	**44**

TROPHIES

Premier League x 2

FA Cup x 2

FA Charity Shield x 1

Kanu had a massive impact here at Arsenal.

ARSÈNE WENGER

This signing is a gamble but one well worth making because of his huge talent. He is a goalscorer as well as a target man, and he can also play the same role as Dennis Bergkamp just behind the main striker, but he is not another Ian Wright. He is more like Alan Smith, who was a key Arsenal player who could hold the ball up and pass it. His problem is that he had so few opportunities at Inter and needs time to come up to his true level again. But we have signed him for four and a half years, and we are prepared to wait to see the best of him.

ARSÈNE WENGER

At times, I didn't play, but I was still the best –
that's how I saw it. If I get 15, 20 minutes, I will do
what I have to do and make an impact.

KANU

I am called a legend, and people see me as one,
but because of that, I don't think I should have to
hide at home and only go on holidays, drink
champagne, and watch TV. I am somebody that
wants to impact on to people's lives.

KANU

CHAPTER

5

THE GREATEST MANAGERS

Arsenal have had many great managers who have brought the club glory and silverware. Whether they left an indelible image by the style their teams played, or the way they managed the players, club and outside world, here are six bosses who have achieved legendary status...

Herbert Chapman
1925 – 1934

A pioneer and the man who put Arsenal among the nation's best clubs, the brilliant Herbert Chapman changed the way managers worked in England and his legacy benefited the Gunners long after his tenure ended.

His revolutionary 3-4-3 system was like nothing ever seen before and his Arsenal team of 1930–31 was one of the best ever, winning the FA Cup in 1930 and the First Division the year after with a club record 127 goals. He would add another league title in 1932–33 before his sudden death in January 1934 aged 55.

The team he built would go on to be crowned champions in 1934 and 1935 to complete a treble of top-flight triumphs in succession.

MANAGERIAL STATS

	PLD	W	D	L
League	359	171	90	98
FA Cup	41	27	7	7
League Cup	0	0	0	0
Europe	0	0	0	0
Other	11	6	0	5
Totals	**411**	**204**	**97**	**110**

TROPHIES

First Division x 2

FA Cup x 1

FA Charity Shield x 3

Did you know?

Master tactician and visionary, Chapman was one of the first managers to invest his players in genuine physical fitness, introducing physiotherapists and masseurs to his team in a bid to give his players an edge. He was also responsible for adding the white sleeves to the previous all-red shirts in 1933.

I am convinced that referees need their help if they are to avoid mistakes and injustices.

HERBERT CHAPMAN

an early advocate for VAR almost 100 years before it became a reality?

Herbert Chapman was integral in the early success of Arsenal Football Club and was an innovator and a pioneer of his time... a magnificent manager.

PETER HILL-WOOD

former Arsenal Chairman

Whoever heard of Gillespie Road?
It is Arsenal around here!

HERBERT CHAPMAN

Gunners boss argues for a tube station name change

Bertie Mee
1966 – 1976

Presiding over 540 games as Gunners boss, Bertie Mee was the first Arsenal manager to win the First Division and FA Cup double.

Mee believed in getting the team off the pitch right before all else and so brought in a backroom staff that included Dave Sexton and Don Howe, then sorting out the team. After installing Frank McLintock as captain, Mee oversaw Arsenal's first major trophy in 17 years when the Inter-Cities Fairs Cup was secured in 1970, and the following year the Double was completed with an unforgettable last day title win at White Hart Lane.

During his 10 years in the Highbury hot-seat, Mee restored the Gunners to being one of the nation's powerhouses once again.

MANAGERIAL STATS

	PLD	W	D	L
League	420	181	115	124
FA Cup	53	25	18	10
League Cup	41	20	11	10
Europe	26	15	4	7
Other	0	0	0	0
Totals	**540**	**241**	**148**	**151**

TROPHIES

First Division x 1

FA Cup x 1

Inter-Cities Fairs Cup x 1

Bertie Mee was a stickler for discipline and other great Arsenal managers, like George Graham, have copied his methods with success.

FRANK McLINTOCK

He didn't like coaching and couldn't do it, yet he had this incredible presence. He didn't let the players get too close, but he was a master of delegating responsibilities to tremendous effect. He was probably a forerunner to most of today's top managers, a wonderful statesmanlike figure.

FRANK McLINTOCK

There was no way we were going to be beaten.

BERTIE MEE

ahead of First Division title decider at Spurs

I'd just like to mention that I've never been so embarrassed by a team's behaviour and our captain was a bloody disgrace to the Arsenal.

BERTIE MEE

unimpressed by his players' drinking on a 1972 tour of Switzerland

Terry Neill

1976 – 1983

Filling Bertie Mee's shoes was never going to be easy, so it felt a little leftfield when the Gunners recruited former player Terry Neill from Spurs in 1976, becoming the club's youngest ever boss at the age of 34 in the process. Neill had spent a decade of his playing career at Highbury and was well-liked on the board.

He would remain in the hot-seat for eight seasons, and while Neill's silverware haul is not that of some of his predecessors, it could be argued that he was the Gunners' greatest "nearly" boss. Neill turned the Gunners into one of the nation's top cup sides, reaching the FA Cup final three times, European Cup Winners' Cup final, as well as two League Cup semi-finals and a top three league finish.

MANAGERIAL STATS

	PLD	W	D	L
League	311	134	87	90
FA Cup	42	40	22	13
League Cup	42	13	9	8
Europe	21	10	5	6
Other	0	0	0	0
Totals	416	187	116	113

TROPHIES

FA Cup x 1

Terry brought me to Arsenal, where he gave me two four-year contracts, and he was also my manager at Spurs. We enjoyed many memorable moments together including four Cup finals – two FA Cups and a European decider. I'm indebted to Terry for the assistance and support he gave me during my career.

PAT JENNINGS

Terry was a colourful character who knew the game. He was a great speaker and could get things across to his players.

PAT JENNINGS

"

Thankfully we had one last moment of glory when Alan Sunderland flew in at the far post and scored the winner with just seconds to go: 3-2 to us. People ask what I felt at the final whistle. Well it was pure relief.

"

TERRY NEILL

on the 1979 FA Cup final

"

In actual fact, it has to be the most amicable sacking in the entire history of association football. I think I had a cup of tea. There was never a fall out. They had to do what they thought was right for the club and I respected that then and I respect that now.

"

TERRY NEILL

George Graham
1986 – 1995

Nine years in the hot-seat, George Graham's reign was one of the best in the club's history, bringing two league titles back to Highbury as well as four other major trophies.

Graham ensured his team was built on a defensive bedrock over fast-flowing, attacking football. The offside trap Graham perfected was the stuff of legend and his astute transfer dealings were also a huge part of his successes – including the purchase of Ian Wright. His investment in the club's youth system, bringing through the likes of Tony Adams and Paul Merson, was also key to a wonderful Gunners side he put together that largely dominated English football for several years.

MANAGERIAL STATS

	PLD	W	D	L
League	350	162	106	82
FA Cup	35	18	9	8
League Cup	53	35	10	8
Europe	19	10	6	3
Other	4	3	1	0
Totals	**461**	**228**	**132**	**101**

TROPHIES

First Division x 2
FA Cup x 1
League Cup x 2
FA Charity Shield x 1

European Cup Winners' Cup x 1

Good back four, everyone behind the ball, good at set plays, very George Graham. No disrespect to Arsène, but George's coaching ability, defensive structure and technical ability, for me, is far better.

TONY ADAMS

George was an outstanding coach – I think I won six or seven trophies under him, including the Cup Winners' Cup against Parma with a team including Ian Selley and David Hillier in midfield and Steve Morrow at the back.

TONY ADAMS

I always think in English football that it's nice to have a combination of different types of players, so then they can all gel together.

GEORGE GRAHAM

That's the only thing I would say that I wanted from all my players: to have that philosophy of hard work when we haven't got [the ball] and perform when we have got it.

GEORGE GRAHAM

Arsène Wenger
1996 – 2018

The greatest Arsenal manager of all-time is one to debate among fans and former players, but Arsène Wenger – to steal one of Brian Clough's lines – must be in the top one! For longevity, trophies won and the beautiful football he presided over, Wenger's legacy made the Gunners one of Europe's best teams for many years, with his ability to find unheard of gems and promote talented youth into polished first team stars is unsurpassed in the club's history.

During an almost 22-year reign, Arsenal won 17 trophies in a style that was thrilling to watch. The boss of the revered "Invincibles", Wenger brought countless superstars to the club and had an uncanny knack of improving almost every one of them. A genius, the like of which may never be seen again.

MANAGERIAL STATS

	PLD	W	D	L
League	828	476	199	153
FA Cup	108	74	20	14
League Cup	73	43	8	22
Europe	216	110	48	58
Other	10	4	5	1
Totals	**1,235**	**707**	**280**	**248**

TROPHIES

Premier League x 3

FA Cup x 7

FA Charity/Community Shield x 7

I think Arsène Wenger is a magnificent physiologist and psychologist. Those are the areas where he excels. He's a lovely man and he has the respect of all the players he's ever worked with.

TONY ADAMS

I'm so grateful to have played for Arsène at this club in my career. He chose me to be one of his players and selected me to be the captain of the club and that's something I will never forget.

MIKEL ARTETA

You can never escape the history of a club like this. At some clubs, success is accidental sometimes – but at Arsenal, it is compulsory.

ARSÈNE WENGER

I dedicated my life to this club – and I'm not scared to say that.

ARSÈNE WENGER

Mikel Arteta

2019 – present day

To include Mikel Arteta in a list of great managers might be a little controversial. By the end of 2024, he'd won just one major trophy – but the foundations he has laid in a relatively short space of time is evidence enough of what Arteta may achieve.

To compete toe to toe with Manchester City – one of the greatest Premier League sides of all time – is a magnificent achievement in itself. Even though the Gunners just fell short twice, the feeling is that year on year a young Arsenal team will learn and eventually get the silverware the fans yearn for. That could be domestically or in Europe – maybe both – but the Arsenal team of today is easy on the eye, dynamic and resilient. Arteta could become one of the club's greatest managers of all time.

MANAGERIAL STATS*

	PLD	W	D	L
League	195	115	36	44
FA Cup	13	8	1	4
League Cup	18	10	3	5
Europe	46	27	10	9
Other	2	0	2	0
Totals	**272**	**160**	**52**	**62**

as of 31/01/2025

TROPHIES

FA Cup x 1

FA Community Shield x 2

[Our relationship] changed because he's in London and I'm in Manchester, so we don't see each other quite often. He's busy, I'm busy, but the affection and the respect I have with him will remain forever, he knows that.

PEP GUARDIOLA

It has surprised me, actually, how detail-oriented he and the whole team are. I've never encountered anything like it, with people who see football that way and who see details as specifically as he does. It can be simple little things or more big things. It's extremely detailed and a lot of little things we talk about, watching video after every game and all that. It's fun working with him and the team. It works.

MARTIN ØDEGAARD

Towards the end of my playing career, I started to speak with Arsène about going into coaching and management myself, and he told me he had already anticipated that. Even the first year when I got here, he said to me, 'One day you are going to be a manager,' and I wasn't really thinking about that at that time.

MIKEL ARTETA

I feel extremely proud, very excited and am looking forward to what is coming next. I feel extremely lucky to work every single day with good people and the ambition we have here. I feel very inspired, I feel challenged, I feel supported, and I want to do much more than what we've already done together.

MIKEL ARTETA

Appearance records

as of 31/01/2025

Most appearances in all competitions:
David O'Leary, 722

Most appearances as a goalkeeper:
David Seaman, 564

Most league appearances: **David O'Leary, 558**

Most FA Cup appearances: **David O'Leary, 70**

Most European appearances:
Thierry Henry, 86

Most consecutive appearances: **Tom Parker, 172**
from 3 April 1926 to 26 December 1929

Youngest first-team player:
Ethan Nwaneri, 15 years, 181 days
against Brentford, Premier League, 18 September 2022

Youngest player to reach 100 appearances:
Cesc Fàbregas, 19 years, 340 days

Oldest first-team player:
Ned Doig, 41 years and 165 days
against Newcastle United, 11 April 1908

Goal-scoring records

as of 31/01/2025

Record goal-scorer: **Thierry Henry, 228**

Most goals in a season: **Ted Drake, 44**
in the 1934–35 season

Most league goals in a season:
Ted Drake, 42
in the First Division, 1934–35

Most FA Cup goals: **Cliff Bastin, 26**

Most European goals: **Thierry Henry, 42**

Fastest goal scored in a match:
Alan Sunderland, 13 seconds
against Liverpool, FA Cup semi-final, second replay, 28 April 1980

Most hat-tricks:
Jack Lambert / Jimmy Brain, 12

Youngest goal-scorer:
Cesc Fàbregas, 16 years, 212 days
against Wolves, League Cup fourth round, 2 December 2003

Oldest goal-scorer:
Jock Rutherford, 39 years, 352 days
against Sheffield United, First Division, 20 September 1924

"

Victoria
Concordia Crescit

"

The Arsenal motto:
Victory Grows Through Harmony